WHAT ARE THEY SAYING ABOUT DOGMA?

What Are They Saying About Dogma?

by
William E. Reiser, S.J.

PAULIST PRESS
New York, N.Y./Ramsey, N.J.

Library of Congress
Catalog Card Number: 78-58955

ISBN: 0-8091-2127-1

Published by Paulist Press
Editorial Office: 1865 Broadway, New York, N.Y. 10023
Business Office: 545 Island Road, Ramsey, N.J. 07446

Printed and bound in the
United States of America

Contents

Preface

Every project has a little history behind it. My interest in the development of dogma began some years ago with a reading of Jean Daniélou's book on Origen. It seemed to me that Origen simply was not a heretic and that he deserved an official place among the saints. Somehow the strictures governing orthodoxy had been too tight, but I had no training in systematic theology to enable me to argue the case.

Heresy was a dirty word. It referred to a willful and woeful separation from the one true fold of Christ. It designated (many of us thought) sundry unintelligible notions in the second and third centuries of the Christian era; it resurfaced in the teachings of the Protestant reformers. But the modern Catholic tended to drop the word heresy from his vocabulary and spoke rather of error and danger. Thus many modern philosophers propagated certain errors (which became apparent, we believed, through a comparison with the philosophy of St. Thomas). Their writings had to be placed on

the Index of Forbidden Books. The biblical studies
which were launched in the nineteenth century contained not only erroneous ideas but dangerous ones
as well. Modernism was the label generically
applied to that wholesale disregard for orthodox,
officially sanctioned doctrine which began with
Alfred Loisy; it epitomized both erroneous thinking
and dangerous teaching. Modernism was heresy
pure and simple.

One difficulty with defining a particular teaching as dogma and contrary teaching as heresy is that
religious truth (unlike the axioms and theorems of
geometry) lives and expands in historical persons.
Thus it is perfectly clear to anyone brought into a
world influenced by Wilhelm Dilthey, Martin
Heidegger, and Hans-Georg Gadamer, that we must
speak in terms of the historicity of truth. For historicity is a basic feature of human beings. It
touches all our acting, thinking, dwelling, feeling. It
profoundly affects the way we grasp and constitute
meaning, as well as the way we search for, discover,
and grow in the truth. God's truth enjoys no exemp-
tion from the laws of historicity either in its incep-
tion (when God reveals himself) or in its reception
(when believers hear the divine address). What
holds for the scriptural word of revelation obtains
for dogma and doctrine too. Truth cannot be regarded as if it existed outside the dimensions of history.

Now the historicity of truth poses a problem for
traditional theology, especially for Roman Catholic
theology. That Christianity is an historical religion

requires that its expression should be liable to change from one age to another. Liturgical practice and piety have assumed a variety of forms down through the centuries; so has the faith itself. Theologians referred to the doctrinal manifestation of this fact by the phrase "the development of dogma."

The heart of the problem (for dogmatic development presents a problem to a religious consciousness that prizes identity and continuity) is briefly this: If dogma is truth and truth is regarded unhistorically, then dogma cannot change essentially; only its mode of expression is open to reformulation. But this creates another problem. Can content and expression be neatly separated such that content becomes independent of expression? As we shall see, such a separation relies heavily on a particular philosophical viewpoint which is not sensitive enough to the way language works. On the other hand, if dogma does develop, how are we to guarantee the sameness of faith through the ages? What are the criteria by which later generations of believers assess the correspondence of their faith with that of the first century? These questions are unavoidable if we take seriously the historicity of truth. The usual but incomplete answer to them is to appeal to authority: to scripture, to tradition, or to an infallible teaching office.

Still, I am not going to pursue the matter of criteriology here. There is, I think, a prior issue, namely, how one is to conceive theologically the nature of dogma and its development. And one curious fact becomes a clue as to why in the course of the history of doctrine someone like Origen is essential and (in very broad strokes) explained: heresy frequently precedes the articulation of dogma. To follow the clue, heresy sometimes resulted from honest speculation, while dogmatic allegiance did not necessarily guarantee good faith. It could be wagered that without heresy there would have been precious little dogmatic development.

The goal then was to come to Origen's defense. To be sure, what a Christian becomes is influenced by his religious convictions, if indeed religious truths actually live in us. In the long run, an error that becomes integrated into one's religious life cannot be helpful. However, in the short run at least, while a mistaken apprehension might warrant a person's being named a heretic, it need not preclude his being counted among the saints either. That depends upon the presence of true charity. Most of us now and again demonstrate a capacity for missing the point, and as our religious convictions are implanted, grow, and take shape, we can expect that at some points in our lives each of us may unwittingly harbor a heresy or two.

But mistakes can be corrected, whether they occur in one's personal religious life or in the corporate life of the Church. Correction happens when convictions are reflected upon and put into words, for then we can ask what the words mean, where the meanings come from, and whether the meanings are truly Catholic.

In attempting to understand what dogma and heresy have meant in the history of doctrine, one discovers that theologians for a long time failed to attend to the nature and extent of pluralism. Dogma and heresy were mutually exclusive. Many a needless battle was waged because of a failure to notice the legitimate variety of viewpoints in the grasp of Christian faith. Pluralism, however, is not a new fact, only a new notion; pluralism has always been around, but its presence and significance seemed rather unimportant until recently. There were a number of reasons for this state of affairs, as we shall see. The medieval theologians realized that many opinions could be marshaled on either side of a particular issue, but according to their scientific ideal (and theology was the sacred science) the truth was ultimately one, not many. Opinions would eventually appear as true or false. That pluralism was a basic feature of the way human beings experience the world and God would have to wait until a later day to be pointed out.

Now that we have acknowledged the place of pluralism, and philosophers have analyzed the way human beings experience the world and have understood somewhat why events are so structured as to make pluralism possible, many people are beginning to wonder where the unity of faith has disappeared. Well, perhaps that unity was frequently more imagined than real. More likely, however, we are simply not accustomed to diversity in religious matters. This situation is a little painful to us, which makes the effort to achieve a contemporary "rule of faith" both pastorally urgent and theologically difficult.

In rehearsing the views of various theologians about dogma, I have limited myself to contemporary Roman Catholic theology; I apologize for not being conversant enough with non-Catholic theology to give these pages a wider readability. Yet it also seems to me that Protestant theology in general has not found the development of dogma to be a *theological* problem, for Protestantism has been more open to the developmental character of religious truth, at least among those for whom dogma is still taken seriously. Nevertheless, development has presented them with some *historical* problems. Protestant theologians have been interested in the emergence of early Catholicism and the history of ecclesiastical doctrines. Many Protestant theologians would agree that dogmas are part of church life.

But the problem of development has been of particular relevance to Catholic theology, I believe, because of our reluctance to appreciate the dogmatic consequences of being historical creatures and because of our Church's insistence upon its historical continuity. Such reluctance has frequently bordered on refusal, but when that happens the road to a solution cannot be along the lines of rational argument. Rather one has to appeal to another's personal experience of faith where the self-revealing God historically and gradually makes himself known to a heart truly prepared to listen.

The aim of this little book is fairly simple. It will attempt to examine what theologians are writing about dogma. But questions can be put to these theologians as to how adequately they have covered the field. That presupposes, I feel, that the present writer has some vantage point of his own from which he draws his questions, sizes up the problems, and points toward a solution. For this reason I want to point out that the pages which follow represent the fallout from a longer, constructive essay on the development of dogma that was happily completed under the direction of Dr. Peter Hodgson at Vanderbilt University. When Paulist Press, at the instigation of my good friend and former teacher, Father Gerald O'Collins, asked me to write *What Are They Saying About Dogma?*, I wondered if I would be able to do the job without explaining at least briefly my own opinion that a more illuminating title might well have been *Whatever Happened to Heresy?* The categories of dogma and heresy are not coordinate. Heresy is a much broader term. Indeed, for centuries it had to be broader because it bore the weight of an uneven grasp of the nature of theological development. As I mentioned earlier, what had been missing was an appreciation of the nature of pluralism in theology. Many teachings were labeled heretical when in fact the issue was whether there must be one and only one way of understanding revealed truth. Anyway, I have added an Appendix to deal with the question of heresy very untechnically, because somewhere I wanted to explain the perspective out of which I view the problem of development in dogma.

Finally, I would like to dedicate these pages with gratitude and deep respect to Bishop James Niedergeses and the priests of the Diocese of Nashville.

The Catholic Center
Nashville, Tennessee
December 8, 1977

1

Development of Dogma as a Theological Question

Let me begin by making two observations. First, if you were to survey the discussion about dogma and the nature of dogmatic development in contemporary Catholic theology, you would find that theologians take two general approaches. The first approach I shall call organic; it tends to focus on the *development* of dogma, which it views as a kind of organic growth process. The second approach is historical-critical; it tends to focus on the development of *dogma,* which it evaluates in terms of a theory of interpretation or hermeneutics. What matters in this approach is the meaning of words, historical circumstances surrounding the origins of a particular dogma, the nature and function of sym-

1

bolic language, and the way the meaning of dogmas is transmitted. Individual theologians might demonstrate both approaches to a greater or lesser degree.

My second observation is this. Every theory of dogmatic development involves two major components. Because dogmas are related to the initial deposit of revelation, a theory of development depends on a theology of revelation. And here you discover that most earlier, pre-Vatican II theologies of revelation described revelation in propositional terms: revelation consisted of those divine truths which God has made known and which the Church, through scripture and conciliar or papal decrees, has enunciated. Vatican II theologies of revelation tended to recapture a biblical perspective. They prefer to regard revelation as an event, that is, as the historical event of God's making himself known to us. Principally, that event occurred in Jesus Christ. But as the gospel is proclaimed and heard in faith the event of revelation, of God encountering us through Christ, continues to happen. Revelation, they claim, is in some sense both closed and ongoing.

The second major component in a theory of dogmatic development is an epistemology or an account of human understanding. Every theology of development, in other words, presupposes a notion of truth. And here you discover that some theologians regard truth as statements which correctly express objective religious facts, while other theologians regard truth as an event. In fact, theologians of the second type are more concerned to talk about meaning: how meaning is constituted, expressed, and transmitted. For them, meaning is a language-event. Meaning "happens" when words are spoken, or are read and understood. Truth, then, is reality as meaningful. This second view is more consistent with an historically sensitive theology than the first view.

We could make a general statement thus: one's theory of knowledge shapes his notion of truth, and one's notion of truth in large measure determines his theology of revelation. The major weakness in a theology of development arises when a theologian wants to talk about revelation as an event but is working (usually without realizing it) with a view of truth as correct propositions about reality. Then the whole dogma business becomes a mess, because the reader is not sure how dogmas (as correct propositions about the faith) and revelation (as the event of God's making himself known to us) are related. It is rather like mixing metaphors.

There is a host of other questions too. Does a dogma clarify what is contained obscurely or implicitly in scripture? Does a dogma have the status of revelation, or is dogma a reflexive articulation of the revelation located in scripture? Is scripture the same thing as revelation, or is revelation a broader notion than scripture alone? After all, the self-revelation of God in Christ was not a written word but *the* spoken word, namely, the person of Jesus Christ. And that utterance preceded the writing of any of our gospels. A dogma is defined (or a creed is formed) under the press of historical questions which may no longer be relevant. Is the later Church stuck with the answers given to questions which are not ours? Or are those answers "classical" such that we are forever bound to them? Are we bound to the answer, to the cultural and linguistic forms in which the answer was expressed, or to both?

If it seems unfair to be bound by the historically and culturally conditioned dogmas of past generations, what about the historical and cultural conditions which influenced the writing of the gospel? Does not the entire Christian faith rest on a particular historical fact, namely, the life and work of Jesus Christ, as well as the Jewish religious tradition out of which he came? Is all belief somehow relative to the situation of each generation of believers, or is there a basic message to which both scripture and the dogmatic tradition are relative?

These are the main questions that prompt theologians to think about dogma. To answer them, as I have said, a theologian will draw on a theology of revelation, a notion of truth, and, it should be added, a theology of the Church, since invariably the discussion leads into the matters of authority, faith, and the guidance of the Holy Spirit.

The Main Line Position

There is a main line, contemporary Roman Catholic position on dogmatic development, and it could be put this way: "The problem of dogmatic development consists basically of the task of demonstrating (as fundamentally possible and in individual cases as really identical) the identity of later, 'evolved' statements of faith with the apostolic statement of revelation which was issued in Christ.''[1] In general, the term "dogma" has come to designate a religious proposition put forward for belief and which carries authority in the community because (1) it has been officially proposed and because (2) it relates fundamentally to New Testament revelation.[2] Dogmas are taken to be immutable. They are like buds off the initial deposit of revelation, and the revelation given us in Jesus Christ (as recorded in the New Testament) is at once fixed, closed, and unchanging. The immutability of dogma has been a peculiarly Catholic position and contrasts with Protestant theology's stance that dogma is relative to gospel.

Now this does not mean that development has nothing to do with dogma; it only means that the locus of development becomes the verbal formulation. The elements to be considered are the cultural, social, and religious influences which call for the translation of ancient and unchanging truths into a new setting. At its simplest form, the main line theory holds that the development of dogma refers to the development of dogmatic formulations; this process is occasioned by the combination of cultural and historical dynamics that move religious history forward. Revelation does not change; only our understanding of it. Sometimes the pattern of development was logical (like the period from Nicea to Chalcedon); at other times it is contingent (there was no dogmatic urgency to proclaim Mary's Assumption). Sometimes development involves a process from the simple apprehension of a revealed truth to a more elaborate statement of what was implicitly contained in the simple, undifferentiated idea. At other times it appears that too much differentiation spoils the basic simplicity and unity of the faith. One begins to wonder whether the sign of a truly developed understanding of the faith is a multiplicity of dogmas or an increased awareness of the basic unity of Catholic belief. The main line theologians are well aware of this problem. In order to rescue the essentially simple and unified nature of the act of faith from being lost in the multiplicity of dogmas, the main line theologians emphasize that revelation is really an event of faith; that faith rests on the unity and simplicity of the person Jesus Christ.

Some Background for the Main Line Position

What are a few of the reasons for this main line position? For one thing, Catholic theologians in general attempt to carry on their work within the parameters of official Church teaching. They rethink our beliefs in contemporary terms and answer new theological questions in ways that remain faithful to the spirit (if not always to the word) of past teaching. Recall, for example, the teaching of Pius IX, given in 1854:

For the Church of Christ, the diligent guardian and champion of the dogmas which have been deposited with her, never changes anything in

them, takes nothing away from them, adds nothing to them; but by handling the ancient dogmas industriously, faithfully, and wisely, if
they have been in any way fashioned from of
old and the faith of the Fathers has engendered
them, she strives so to polish and refine them
that those venerable dogmas of heavenly teaching receive the distinctness of language, light,
clarification, but retain their fullness, purity,
uniqueness, and that they might increase in one
way only, namely, as the same dogma, with the
same understanding, and with the same intention.[3]

Again, the oath against modernism, issued by Pius
X in 1910, reads in part:

I sincerely hold that the doctrine of faith was
handed down to us from the apostles through
the orthodox Fathers in exactly the same meaning and always in the same purport. Therefore,
I entirely reject the heretical misinterpretation
that dogmas evolve and change from one meaning to another different from the one which the
Church held previously.[4]

The unmistakable intention of the papal statements was to exclude development from touching
the content of revealed truth: "Any meaning of the
sacred dogmas that has once been declared by Holy
Mother Church, must always be retained; and there
must never be any deviation from that meaning on

the specious grounds of a more profound understanding."[5]

But the main line position, I feel, has not been
framed just out of obedience to the teaching office
of the Church. Rather, it follows from a pervasive
Catholic sense that modern faith must be apostolic
in the vital sense of that word. In the phrasing of the
First Eucharistic Prayer, it must always be "the
faith that comes to us from the apostles." What the
Church "believes, teaches, and confesses on the
basis of the word of God" (as Jaroslav Pelikan puts
it) must remain the same throughout the ages if the
Church is to remain truly apostolic and catholic.

And here is the problem. How can we reconcile
immutability and development? To claim that development refers to the formulation but not to the
content of dogma places one at odds with Cardinal
Newman, for his theory (whatever its inadequacies)
was constructed to explain how the Church could
maintain its identity over time even though it had
"added" new dogmas. How are later dogmas continuous with the ancient faith? Are there not some
dogmas (such as the Immaculate Conception) that
are extremely difficult to locate in the original deposit of revelation?

The question about continuity has certain
presuppositions. Continuity needs to be established
historically. In the first place, the history of dogma
was not a purely logical development; thus the continuity between generations of Christians may often
be hard to demonstrate. An orthodox belief perhaps
owes as much to political, social, and geographical

factors as to theological ones. For the sake of political unity and religious concord, Constantine had a stake in Nicea's reaching a common formula about the divinity of Christ. The fact that Trent issued its decrees in a religiously polemical atmosphere while Vatican II did not may account for the somewhat slow arrival of a defense of religious liberty.

In the second place, while we do look for and experience genuine continuity from one age to another, our human lives are filled with the experiences of novelty. Dogmatic development touches upon a very ancient philosophical question, namely, whether reality is to be explained in terms of identity and continuity (Parmenides) or in terms of novelty and flux (Heraclitus). We experience both of these things in our lives. The attempt to draw up a philosophical account of the matter is tough enough; to render a theological account is harder still. And so, underlying the problem of the development of dogma is the very broad philosophical question about how anything that is alive manifests both sameness and difference. Growth is a dynamic process; a theology of development therefore deals with the dynamics at work in the historical unfolding of the Christian faith.

There is another possible reason why the general Catholic position on development has assumed its present form, and that is the reaction against Modernism. In the wake of nineteenth-century idealist philosophy some theologians had proposed a theory of dogmatic development which viewed development as a necessary feature in the ontological structure of reality. Revelation too necessarily undergoes development, and thus dogma has the status of new revelation. This was exemplified by the Protestant theologian Ferdinand Christian Baur. Baur described development as an historical process whereby the "one implicit dogma" increasingly differentiates itself; the Absolute Truth becomes more clear to us through the activity of thinking.[6] This view is Hegelian. Whatever its flaws, the idealist view does provide a theological account for the fact that Christian faith has not been expressed in the twentieth century as it was in the first. But since continuity with the ancient faith ruled any novelty out of the question, and since Hegelian philosophy was suspect, an idealist approach to dogmatic development would have failed. Besides, contemporary theologians like Avery Dulles, Bernard Lonergan, and Karl Rahner have stressed that dogmatic development does not proceed according to a priori laws. Our grasp of revelation need not become increasingly differentiated; it could become increasingly unified and simple.

Some nineteenth-century Catholic theologians appealed to a tradition principle in order to explain how the faith could be historically continuous while in the process of developing (John Adam Möhler, Cardinal Newman, and Maurice Blondel, for instance). They worked with the idea that the Church was a living organism animated by the Holy Spirit; like all organisms, it would grow and change. Johannes Kuhn, another Tübingen theologian, believed that dogmatic development resulted from the dialectic of orthodox and heretical forces. He wrote, with an Hegelian tone, that "faith develops, of itself, dialectically. Christian dogma is the objective mind of the Christian consciousness."[7]

Summary

One could say that there are two general approaches to the problem of dogmatic development. One approach is by way of an organic model. It was adopted by the Catholic Tübingen theologians (Möhler and Kuhn) and Cardinal Newman. Essentially they conceived the nature of an idea in organic terms, subject to laws of growth similar to organic development. Jan Walgrave is a contemporary spokesman for this view. A variation on this basic view consists of distinguishing expression and content. What is permanent and unchanging in a dogma is its content or meaning; what develops is its linguistic expression. This view is Aristotelian, grounded in the form-matter distinction. Dogma does not undergo substantial change (in the case of dogma, its meaning is its substance) because substantial change would amount to corruption. Bernard Lonergan takes this view; so does Avery Dulles, as well as a number of recent official Church statements. A still further refinement turns along more idealist lines, though it clearly lies along the same trajectory as Newman and Lonergan. Karl Rahner is its chief architect. His treatment, combining philosophy and theology, is the most comprehensive.

The second general approach is hermeneutical.

Rejecting entirely or else critically restating some of the epistemological presuppositions of the organic model, proponents of this approach are searching for ways to reformulate the meaning of ecclesiastical dogmas. Their hermeneutical principles lead them away from the organic model because it has not done full justice to the historicity of truth. Leslie Dewart and Hans Küng are spokesmen for this view. Yet there are important variations on this approach. Walter Kasper shifts the problem of development so that it becomes almost exclusively theological. Others reject the content versus expression distinction as too facile and unfaithful to the way language functions. They readily grant the fact of development and concentrate on the task of making dogmatic meaning contemporary. Piet Schoonenberg, Thomas Ommen, and to a degree Gerald O'Collins, represent this move.

In the next two chapters we shall look at these general approaches, and in the fourth chapter evaluate them. It could be noted that Kasper, Schoonenberg, Ommen, and O'Collins are more concerned with the notion of dogma than with the notion of development. But no one writes about dogma unless he finds it somewhat of a theological bother, and the bother generally boils down to a tension between truth as fixed and truth as growing. What follows merely sketches the discussion going on in contemporary Catholic theology. Often enough solutions overlap. Nor have I attempted to be inclusive of everyone writing about dogma. A more extensive treatment of the history of thinking about dogmatic development can be found elsewhere.[8]

Finally, the words dogma and doctrine are often used interchangably. The term dogma has become a technical theological expression only within the last hundred years or so. The truths of the faith which carried high authority would have appeared in the form of a creed, or have been referred to as the "rule of faith" or (with the medievals) as "articles of faith." Or the truths might have been qualified by theological notes, such as "of the Catholic faith," or "defined," or "theologically certain." Doctrine, however, does not connote the same degree of authority as dogma. While both words refer to meanings or truths that have been set into propositions, doctrine is more inclusive. Doctrine might designate particular teachings which are less solemnly proclaimed (what Dulles has called "secondary truths"). For example, we speak of the doctrines of purgatory and free will. Or doctrine might designate (as I think it should) what the Church teaches as it goes about its business of proclaiming the gospel; it may not always be as specifically articulated as a dogmatic pronouncement. In this sense, to talk about the development of *doctrine* is to talk about a whole complex of things; it is to talk about the Church's historically conditioned growth in understanding all the gospel's dimensions.

Footnotes to Chapter 1

1. Karl Rahner and Karl Lehmann, "Geschichtlichkeit der Vermittlung," *Mysterium Salutis,*

Band I, *Die Grundlagen heilsgeschichtlicher Dogmatik* (Einsiedeln, Zürich, Cologne, 1965), p. 728.

2. On the concept of dogma in Catholic theology, see Thomas Ommen, *The Hermeneutic of Dogma* (Montana, 1975), pp. 61-72.

3. Denzinger-Schönmetzer (1965), 2802.

4. *DS* 3541. Translation appears in *The Church Teaches* (St. Louis, 1955), p. 37.

5. *DS* 3020 *(The Church Teaches*, p. 34).

6. Peter C. Hodgson, *Ferdinand Christian Baur: On the Writing of Church History* (New York, 1968), pp. 276-77, 297, 364.

7. Elmar Klinger, "Tübingen School," *Sacramentum Mundi* (New York, 1970), vol. 6, p. 319.

8. For example, see Jan Walgrave, *Unfolding Revelation* (Philadelphia, 1972) or Georg Söll, *Dogma und Dogmenentwicklung* (Freiburg, 1971).

2
The Organic View
of Development

The story began with John Adam Möhler and
John Henry Newman in the nineteenth century.
Möhler approached dogmatic development through
his ecclesiology, while Newman started with an
epistemology. One adopted an organic model of the
Church and the other an organic model of how ideas
develop. While both men played an influential role
in the currents of twentieth century theology,
Newman has had a stronger effect on theologies of
development.

The central feature in Möhler's ecclesiology
was the unity of the Church. He saw all the external
features of the Church (its structure, piety, doctrines, etc.) forming a coherent unity like the topog-
raphy of a living organism; its life principle is the
Holy Spirit. The external features develop, that is,
they grow and assume increasingly definite shapes

and contours. Development reflects "the necessary becoming-body of the Spirit."[1] Dogmas are rational expressions of the Church's inner life; they represent the Church's growing consciousness of its inner unity. Therefore, though there are many dogmas, they arise from a single source (the Holy Spirit). While on one level development reveals a multiplicity of dogmas, on another level they stem from and point toward an inner unity and simplicity. Möhler's theology of development admitted the need for tradition, authority, and a distinction between the substance of the original revealed doctrine and the form of its expression.

Rahner's theology resembles Möhler's, as we shall see, in that Rahner situates the problem of development within an overall grasp of the nature and unity of the Church. Dogmatic development thus becomes an ecclesiological matter, not merely an epistemological one; it is to be understood against the background of the mystery of the Church.

Newman explained that the Church of his day could legitimately claim to be apostolic because growth is a characteristic of living things, and living things grow in ways that are consonant with their inner constitution. Christianity is a real idea and ideas are living. The idea of Christianity includes all the possible aspects about the original revelation; no single aspect exhausts its content. Consider, he suggests, how the mind receives an idea as an undifferentiated impression; it germinates and matures, sometimes through deduction and inference, at

other times subconsciously as experience widens
and further impressions are received. The same
idea may be entertained in different ways by different minds. Thus ideas have their social histories and
can be modified by their surroundings. Ideas, as
Whitehead said in our own time, have their adven-
tures. Consequently, Newman wrote:

> If Christianity is a fact, and impresses an idea
> of itself on our minds and is a subject-matter of
> exercises of the reason, that idea will in course
> of time expand into a multitude of ideas, and
> aspects of ideas, connected and harmonious
> with one another, and in themselves determi-
> nate and immutable, as is the objective fact it-
> self which is thus represented.[2]

In the celebrated distinction from his *Grammar
of Assent*, Newman introduced the phrases "notional apprehension" and "real apprehension." Notional apprehension designated the conceptual
grasp, analysis, and expression of an idea; real apprehension referred to the mind's penetrating an
idea so that idea came alive in the fabric of one's
conscious life. The depth, liveliness, and historical
development of an idea depend upon an apprehension that is real; Christianity is a real idea.

Revelation occurred as an original wordless
impression upon the minds and hearts of the apostles; the expansion of that idea and its explication
are moments in a continuous organic life process
which proceeds under the direction of the Holy

Spirit. True development, therefore, is guaranteed by the Spirit; but the social reality of the Church requires the presence of a voice that can definitively distinguish development from corruption. The Church as a whole may have a feeling for the truth, but as a whole the Church does not know how to formulate it.

There are some ambiguities, however, in Newman's approach. Were the apostles at a disadvantage compared to later generations of Christians because their grasp of the idea of Christianity was not so differentiated as ours? Does the believer today also receive an idea of Christianity, however dim or unclarified, in its wholeness? Is revelation to be compared to a seed that is planted and later matures, or to an idea? In other words, shall we conceive of revelation in organic fashion or as a number of propositions? Newman seems to have been operating with a dual view of revelation.

The broad lines of Lonergan's treatment of dogmatic development are similar to Newman's, as we shall see. For Lonergan, the development of dogma is a question connected with theological method, and theological method grows out of his cognitional theory. In his account of dogmatic development (*Unfolding Revelation*, 1972), Jan Walgrave put together (1) Newman's view of ideas with an existentialist twist and (2) the personalist attitude toward revelation (God communicates *himself*) which the Church had appropriated at the Second Vatican Council with "The Dogmatic Constitution on Divine Revelation." Revelation, the Council taught, consists primarily of the event of God's sharing himself; secondarily it consists of the statements describing that event. That decree was an advance upon the propositionally minded view of revelation taken by Vatican I.

Borrowing Newman's distinction between notional and real apprehension, Walgrave argues that notional apprehension yields theoretical truth, whereas real apprehension touches life and involves a deep-seated grasp of what human existence means. While theoretical truth is usually expressed through concepts and definitions, existential truth is communicated through image and symbol. Revelation, according to Walgrave, is a special kind of existential truth mediated to us through symbols, images, and religious language. If God's truth reaches men through language, then that language must be heard under grace. The pre-condition of graced hearing is change of heart; and thus the real cause of a person's hearing God's truth addressed to him in human words is the Holy Spirit.

For Walgrave, dogmatic development begins with the conceptualization processes of the human mind. God's saving truth is present to us as a whole, even though our conscious apprehension of it may be partial. Under the natural impulse to clarify ideas we understand more thoroughly the reality which is globally present to us. "What appears to man in the light of faith is always complete and perfect, but his existential apprehension of it is always imperfect because his spiritual eye is weak."[3] Notional and real apprehension of God's revelation should not be divorced, however. Religion needs the symbols and images of faith and the symbolic language of scripture, and the more technical language of conceptual expression. Genuine development involves both a clearer and a deeper grasp of divine truth; depth keeps clarity from becoming selective.

The believer has received, then, an intuitive awareness of saving reality as a whole insofar as God has made himself present in one's life. God's message, which scripture embodies, is continually re-heard within a living tradition. Development amounts to a progressive analysis of an idea present to us in its wholeness. "In itself, the development of doctrine is a process of discursive thought, or of reasoning, if you like, but in the broadest sense of the word."[4] The point of departure is God's revelation as located in the words of scripture, but Walgrave reminds us that scriptural words hold a "fuller sense" than what verbal statements in the Bible seem to express. The fuller meaning of the scriptural words unfolds through the ages:

> The whole truth that is immediately present to man in the light of faith is entirely signified by the scriptural Word although it is not entirely rendered by its verbal translation.[5]

Expression versus content

> The substance of the ancient doctrine of the deposit of faith is one thing, and the way in which it is presented is another (Pope John XXIII).

Furthermore, while adhering to the methods and requirements proper to theology, theologians are invited to seek continually for more suitable ways of communicating doctrine to the men of their times. For the deposit of faith or revealed truths are one thing; the manner in which they are formulated without violence to their meaning and significance is another ("The Pastoral Constitution on the Church in the Modern World" #62).

There is a widely shared view that frames dogmatic development as an issue of expression and content. You find this view shared by theologians like Avery Dulles, Bernard Lonergan, Prudence DeLetter, as well as by Church documents of a Vatican II vintage.[6] Behind this view were a number of influences. Since the turn of the century, theologians have paid greater attention to the historical character of knowledge, that is, how history affects our way of thinking, our language, even our understanding of human nature. Words that carried one meaning many centuries ago might carry a different meaning today. An old formulation may be venerable, but it may not be pastorally beneficial for explaining the faith today. Another influence, which I alluded to in the Preface, is the modern Church's awareness of pluralism. The Second Vatican Council in some ways reflected the Church's pastoral response to the problems created by this awareness. Pluralism means that cultural and social differences cannot be ignored by a Church whose message is intended for all the nations. It means too that there will be a variety of perspectives and conceptual frameworks in which the gospel message will be listened to, understood, and expressed. And this variety began in the New Testament itself.

This brings us to a third influence. I think it is still very hard to estimate the impact of the biblical explosion that has taken place over the past three decades. Virtually every dimension of Catholic theology has been profoundly affected by our better understanding of scripture, so much so that nearly every theologian today in some way will incorporate a biblical perspective or else will be relying on his assimilation of a biblical perspective. Dogmatic development has become both an epistemological problem (how does truth evolve and yet remain the same?) and a kerygmatic one (how shall we proclaim the ancient faith so that it speaks to people of today?). In other words, not only are we trying to figure out how to reformulate our dogmas; we are also attempting to preach and explain the revealed word of God. And we have found that the word of scripture did not always mean what we thought it meant. That is why theologies of revelation and theologies of development have something in common; systematic theologians and scriptural theologians are involved in the task of interpreting the word of God for today.

Bernard Lonergan devoted considerable attention to the difference between classical and modern notions of culture, for this difference bears directly on the manner in which theology is practiced today.[7] This difference, he pointed out, underlies modern theology's concern with pluralism, and pluralism highlights some of the problems associated with dogmatic development.

First, Lonergan distinguishes the original message of faith from the early Church doctrines. Doctrines are expressions of meaning. As such, doctrines help to define what the community of faith is all about; they establish the boundaries of the community's shared belief; and because they emerge out of a process of reflection, doctrines serve as the reflective formulas through which ancient teaching is communicated from one generation of believers to another. Doctrines are authentic (and not merely formal) declarations of belief if they are based upon conversion, because the converted heart is in touch with the foundational reality of Christian faith. Doctrines become inauthentic to the degree that a tradition becomes faithless either by deviating from the genuine meaning of its doctrines or by selectively ignoring them.

Second, doctrines are statements, statements are meaningful within a context, and contexts are ongoing. A doctrine that comes out of one cultural and historical setting cannot be transposed into a different time and culture without taking account of all the differences between them. Otherwise, one may proclaim as part of the ancient faith what is just the relative, accidental feature of a particular historical situation. How will the Church determine what features are relative and which are ancient and essential? Ultimately, this task falls to theologians; their success will depend upon whether they are truly converted and therefore in touch with the basic reality of faith, which is Jesus Christ.

Third, the reason why the basic message of revelation will be received, understood, and expressed in many different ways is the fact that human consciousness is differentiated in so many different manners. Some people are poets and artists, some scholars and scientists, some farmers and housewives, and so forth. This means that men and women see the world from a wide variety of perspectives. But what is true for individuals also holds true for an entire culture or historical period. One age is marked by its perception of reality in terms of the sacred and profane; another by its critical, scientific world view. Another by its interest in interiority and philosophical reflection. Some ages record the past through myth, story, and saga; another through a detailed recounting of facts. The Fathers of the Church wondered about the divinization of man; the Church of Vatican II wonders about his humanization. Differentiations of consciousness, therefore, make pluralism inevitable. But they also play a part in the development of dogma.

Differentiation of consciousness can affect an entire culture. Lonergan refers to this process as the ongoing discovery of mind. Within this process there are ongoing contexts, which is one way of describing how dogma (and doctrines) develop:

Ongoing context arises when a succession of texts express the mind of a single historical community. Such an ongoing context necessitates a distinction between prior and subsequent context. Thus a statement may intend to deal with one issue and to prescind from other, further issues. But settling one does not burke the others. Usually it contributes to a clearer grasp of the others and to a more urgent pressure for their solution. According to Athanasius the council of Nicea used a non-scriptural term, not to set a precedent, but to meet an emergency. But the emergency lasted for some thirty-five years and, some twenty years after it had subsided, the first council of Constantinople felt it necessary to answer in a non-technical manner whether only the Son or also the Holy Spirit was consubstantial with the Father. Fifty years later at Ephesus, it was necessary to clarify Nicea by affirming that it was one and the same that was born of the Father and also born of the Virgin Mary. Twenty-one years later it was necessary to add that one and the same could be both eternal and temporal, both immortal and mortal, because he had two natures. Over two centuries later there was added the further clarification that the divine person with two natures also had two operations and two wills.[8]

Such is the meaning of an ongoing context, but

Lonergan notes that not all development proceeds in the same way. Issues that were not relevant to the New Testament writers became important for the philosophically differentiated consciousness of the early medieval world. On the other hand, the dogmas that emerged from Trent, or the Marian dogmas of 1854 and 1950, cannot be situated within the logic of an ongoing context like that of the christological statements.

Finally, for Lonergan dogmas and doctrines are distinct. Dogma connotes a permanence of meaning which results from the fact that dogmas arise in order to express, however inadequately, revealed mysteries. He prefers to speak of the permanence rather than the immutability of dogma because what the Church wants to maintain is not so much immutable formulas but those divinely revealed truths whose meaning (not the verbal formulation of the meaning) is forever binding. Immutability sounds too much like the assumptions of classicist culture which believed you could nail down a doctrine in words that would always express the same thing.[9]

Lonergan and Newman have a common interest in the way ideas develop, how they are received in the mind, are shaped and expand. I have called their approaches organic because they are concerned with the growth and expansion of ideas, and because the central part of their thinking about dogmatic development concentrates on the ways in which divinely communicated truths germinate and mature. For Lonergan, the undifferentiated content of revelation undergoes a reflective differentiation and is open to many different expressions. I would like to suggest, however, that what matters is not *how* dogma develops, or rather, *in what manner* the deposit of revelation unfolds. For to view the question from an epistemological point seems to make the whole business so rationalistic. What matters more is how a revelation once given (and definitively given) continues to meet later generations of believers. In other words, if dogma is not related to God's ongoing revelation (however we explain it) here and now, then a person could conclude that dogmas really are not important. Scripture is important, because that is where the permanent meanings are somehow located. Unless dogma is related to a theology of revelation, what prevents us from seeing dogma simply as the expression of an unchanging content (the revelation secured in scripture)? Then, because expression is relative to content, Christianity could be "de-dogmatized."

Karl Rahner and Dogmatic Development

Rahner is probably the most important Catholic theologian of our time. His account of dogmatic development is theological in the full sense of the word. Rahner draws upon his theological anthropology, his theology of revelation and history, and his theology of the Church. While we cannot examine each of these issues in detail, we shall say enough about them to gather Rahner's main idea about dogmatic development.

First of all, Rahner understands revelation as an event and not as a set of propositions from which

dogmas can be deduced. Revelation is the word of
God, that is, his total saving message. This message
is actualized when the word of God is proclaimed
and responded to. The proclamation occurs out of a
living tradition and within the community of faith.
Scripture tells us how God has revealed himself, but
the event of God's meeting us here and now depends upon the gospel's proclamation and its reception by faith.[10] Scripture and revelation are thus
distinguished, for God's revealing action preceded
the composition of the New Testament writings. In
this way revelation holds a priority over the word of
scripture; revelation designates God's self-
communication which no written word can adequately contain.

Now, in the early Church there did exist a rule
of faith which preceded the writing of scripture and
afterward guided the constitution and selection of
the New Testament canon. Rahner calls this "a
dogmatic moment."[11] This is consistent with his
theological anthropology:

> there is a transcendental necessity for man as
> mind and spirit (and consequently for every
> human society) to affirm certain truths abso-
> lutely . . . . Consequently, man's existence is
> essentially a "dogmatic" one.[12]

The Church therefore needs to affirm certain truths
definitively because they pertain so intrinsically to
its identity and mission. Such truths are immutable.
The history of dogma amounts to the historical ad-

ventures of the unchanging truths as they are proclaimed, understood, received, translated into suitable idioms, and handed on. While they appear to
be numerous, dogmas comprise a unity that is based
on the unity and totality of faith, which is God himself. This unity is what makes possible the historical
continuity of faith. A proper understanding of dogmatic development devolves on this underlying continuity, for the later expressions of belief must have
been potentially present in the earlier ones:

> The solution of the problem (very formally and
> very generally stated) must be sought for in the
> fact that a new dogma is contained "implicitly"
> in an old dogma or in the totality of earlier
> things which have been believed.[13]

Some precision is called for. You cannot reduce
the process of development to establishing the logical connections among the basic truths of faith, or
of reaching inferences from those truths. An
abstract, timeless system of belief does not exist
somewhere waiting to be unpacked. Historical process is free and undetermined, and so the course of
development may at times appear logical and at
other times accidental. This does not rule out, however, a movement from the implicit to the explicit.
Theological questioning, for example, brings dogmatic implications to light.

Now what is so theological about this process?
Rahner claims that new truths have originated from
God's initial revelation. Although the founding

events of revelation are concluded, the history of
faith is open, since the ways in which later believers
hear the gospel are historically conditioned. Therefore, Rahner can insist that grace also has a history;
the conferral of grace in every age necessarily re-
spects the historical situation of that age.[14] But only
God confers grace. It is his work. Therefore, if the
history of faith (and thus the development of
dogma) depends on grace, then the initiative in
dogmatic development also belongs to God. And
that is why the process is theological.

Secondly there is an ecclesial dimension to development. Dogmatic statements make objective
truth-claims which are mediated by the community
of faith, that is, by the Church. In other words,

> the Church reflects on the message—given by
> and received from Jesus Christ and transmitted
> in the belief of the primitive Church—in relation
> to each particular, historically conditioned situ-
> ation and based on her consciousness of faith
> and its original source. She reflects on this mes-
> sage and proclaims the one permanent faith
> anew in the form of this new theological reflec-
> tion, in such a way that this faith retains and
> acquires once more as inevitable a presence as
> possible for the one who hears the message of
> the Church to make a decision.[15]

All dogmatic formulations presuppose the original
historical event of revelation which forever binds
future generations of Christians. Dogmas are not
ends in themselves; they always refer to and ex-

plicate something beyond themselves, namely, the self-communication of God.

A number of points need to be mentioned regarding the dynamics of development as an event in the life of the Church:

(1) The hearer of revelation undergoes a supernatural elevation by grace. He listens to words and is enabled (by grace) to hear the voice of God in them. The Holy Spirit activates our hearing so that the meaning we perceive is acknowledged to be God speaking to us.

(2) The Church and its magisterium do not mediate a revelation that is being spoken for the first time each time it is proclaimed. They do proclaim, with a living voice, however, because revelation is happening now. Magisterium does not initiate the process of development; history is responsible for that.

(3) Words express what we mean, that is, our ideas and concepts; words make it possible for us to think and to make our thinking precise. Dogmatic development allows religious consciousness to express and make precise what it has experienced. In other words, there would be no dogmatic development (and no theology) unless we were rational beings.

(4) Tradition is the mode by which the past survives into the present. We do not read scripture as if it were written only yesterday. As members of an historical community of faith, we hear the gospel as announced to us through the faith of the past.

(5) The dogmas of the Church are part of re-

vealed truth. In enunciating them the Church realizes that they form part of the original revelation. The difficult question about how a proposition which has never been consciously and reflexively affirmed can exist within the totality of faith has to be answered by appealing to the *fides ecclesiastica*.[16]

In the third place, revelation closed with the end of the apostolic generation, for that generation experienced Jesus Christ as the definitive event which interprets for us the meaning of history.[17] The crucial question for a theology of development is to ask how dogmas relate to that event. Sometimes, as we saw, later dogmas appear because they were implied in earlier statements of belief. But Rahner believes that dogmatic development can start from an experience as well as from a proposition.

The apostles enjoyed a global experience of Jesus in his earthly and in his risen life. That experience underlies all of their statements about him. Thus revelation takes place on two levels: (1) the relation between the experience of the apostles and their verbal expression of that experience, and (2) the relation between their proclamation and the scriptures (which they did not personally compose). In other words, beneath the scriptural words lies the experience that led the apostles to preach and to witness, and which inspired another generation to put it into words. Rahner writes:

Every explication which has been successfully established in propositional form illuminates the original experience, allows it to grow to its proper stature, and becomes an intrinsic factor in the abiding life of this experience itself.[18]

The explicit statement, therefore, is connected with its underlying experience in such a way that it is both more than and less than that experience. Yet we too have the gift of the Spirit. And so post-apostolic development also begins (as it did with the apostles) with "what is implicit as a living possession of the whole truth in an unreflexive but conscious way."[19]

Summary and Transition

Cardinal Newman adopted an organic approach to development as he tried to explain how Christianity, considered as a real idea, could expand and differentiate without undergoing substantial change. Lonergan follows that trajectory. For him the process of development is explained by ongoing contexts and differentiations of consciousness. Rahner's global experience which reflexively unfolds through propositions appears to lie on the same path as Newman's idea of Christianity. With Newman, Rahner insists on the guidance of the Holy Spirit and the need for a teaching authority as elements in a theology of development. Like Lonergan, Rahner recognized that the permanence of dogma must be distinguished from its conceptual expression. Where Lonergan appealed to differentiations of consciousness in order to explain how the same meaning is appropriated in different ways at different times and places, Rahner spoke of the history of grace which emerges from the way revelation is subjectively heard by individual believers.

All organic model theologians have served up variations on the major recurring problem, namely, how later expressions are related to primitive experience. Their basic point of agreement is that living things grow without surrendering their identity. The issue that meets us next is the relation between expression and experience, between dogma and gospel. But it is an issue that calls for a different approach to the basic problem of development.

Footnotes to Chapter 2

1. Hans Geisser, *Glaubeneinheit and Lehrentwicklung bei Johann Adam Möhler* (Göttingen, 1971), p. 43.

2. John Henry Newman, *An Essay on the Development of Christian Doctrine* (Westminster, Md., 1968 [reprint of the 1878 edition]), p. 55.

3. Jan Walgrave, *Unfolding Revelation* (Philadelphia, 1972), p. 373.

4. Ibid., p. 378.

5. Ibid., p. 381; cf. also pp. 346-46.

6. P. DeLetter, S.J., "Note on the Reformability of Dogmatic Formulas," *The Thomist* 38 (1974), 747-53; Avery Dulles, *The Survival of Dogma* (New York, 1971), p. 160ff.; Raymond Brown, *Biblical Reflections on Crises Facing the Church* (New York, 1975), pp. 3-19. Also, The Sacred Congregation for Catholic Education, "The Theological Formation of Future Priests" (Rome, 1976), #33. The Holy Father has made this point a number of times. See, for example, "Apostolic Exhortation to all the Bishops in Peace and Communion with the Apostolic See, on the fifth Anniversary of the Close of the Second Vatican Council," *The Teachings of Paul VI–1970* (Washington, D.C., 1971), p. 469.

7. Bernard Lonergan, *A Second Collection* (Philadelphia, 1974), pp. 1-9, 55-67, 101-116, 149-163.

8. Lonergan, *Method in Theology* (New York, 1972), p. 313.

9. Ibid., pp. 323-326.

10. Karl Rahner and Karl Lehmann, *Kerygma and Dogma* (New York, 1969), p. 15ff.

11. Ibid., p. 78.

12. Rahner, "Dogma," *Sacramentum Mundi* (New York, 1968), vol. 2, p. 95.

13. Rahner-Lehmann, *Mysterium Salutis*, vol. 1, pp. 731-32.

14. Ibid., p. 732.

15. Rahner, "What is a Dogmatic Statement?" *Theological Investigations"* (New York, 1975), vol. 5, p. 53.

16. Rahner, "Considerations on the Development of Dogma," *Theological Investigations,* vol. 4, pp. 12-20.

17. Rahner, "The Development of Dogma," *Theological Investigations,* vol. 1, pp. 48-49.

18. Ibid., p. 66.

19. Ibid., p. 68.

3

The Historical-Critical View of Development

A number of theologians tackle the problem of dogmatic development by situating the Church's dogmas within their original context. Then they proceed to ask about the relevance of a given dogma to contemporary faith. This leads to some interesting results.

The meaning of a dogma might be relativized to a particular time and place, e.g., to the time of Nicea. The conditions from which the dogma arose were peculiar to the situation of the fourth century but are no longer relevant. Or, considering dogma as man-made propositions about divine revelation, a theologian could try to relate dogma as propositional to the gospel as the experience which makes any faith-propositions possible. Thus, what becomes important is not so much the Nicene formula as the Church's experience of Jesus Christ through which it knows that Jesus is God's Son alive and glorious. Or, attending to the historical roots of a given dogma, a theologian might develop hermeneutical principles by which contemporary believers understand what the dogma should mean to them. Or, a theologian might be led to question whether the category "dogma" is pastorally helpful. The concept of dogma is perhaps too inflexible for the Church's catechetical mission today. Let us look at these results more closely.

The Historicization of Dogma

Several years ago, Leslie Dewart and Bernard Lonergan locked horns over the merits and demerits of the notion of truth which lay behind Greek philosophy and scholastic metaphysics. The bulk of Lonergan's work had involved him in appropriating St. Thomas' theory of knowledge. Lonergan realized that not only was St. Thomas' theory based on universal features of human knowing, but his theory could be verified by modern thinkers who attended carefully to their own acts of understanding. Dewart argued, however, that Greek philosophy and scholastic metaphysics were based on a Greek notion of truth—a notion that was neither universal nor transcendental, but peculiar to a specific culture.

Dewart rejected Lonergan's position as well as that broader movement in twentieth century Catholic thought known as transcendental Thomism; he was convinced that Western philosophy, and particularly scholastic metaphysics, were considerably more Greek than gospel. The theology which has emerged from that tradition is culturally biased; what is called for is a dehellenization of dogma. Dewart was providing a systematic base for Adolph Harnack's thesis that dogma was a Greek invention on the soil of the gospel. The place where this becomes most apparent is the Greek notion of truth.

If I could put the matter technically for a moment, the terms of the debate went like this. Lonergan contended that the Aristotelian notion of truth as appropriated by St. Thomas was rooted not in Greek culture but in the structure of human understanding. Furthermore, the structure of understanding is a universal feature of human being. A person can become reflectively aware of that structure by noticing the way he experiences, understands, judges, and decides. Truth on this scheme is an affirmation of what is so. The converse of the notion of truth is the notion of being. Just as truth is grounded in the transcendental features of human understanding, so is being. The link connecting truth and being is the notion of intelligibility.

Dewart based his rejection of the scholastic notions of truth and being on the fact that they did not square with an adequate account of human consciousness. According to the scholastics, Dewart said, truth is immutable because it consists of the mind's conformity to an object of thought (an object that always remains the same).[1] When applied to a theory of dogmatic development, the scholastic view would reduce all later dogmas to the original

scriptural statements; the faith must ever remain the
same, immutable, and closed to real development.
But in actual fact, do not dogmas represent an advance upon the original statements? Do they not say
something that was not said before? If you pay attention to the ongoing development of human consciousness, Dewart answered, then you must say
yes:

> Truth is not the adequacy of our representative
> operations, but the adequacy of our conscious
> existence. More precisely, it is the fidelity of
> consciousness to being.[2]

For Dewart, then, truth is not so much a
straightforward correspondence of mind and thing
(because this is such a static conception of truth) as
the living relation between our consciousness and
the world around us. Truth continually emerges
from the ongoing differentiation of our conscious
experience, and therefore truth, no more than existence, can always remain the same.[3]

The truth of Christian beliefs consists in the
effectiveness of those beliefs in relating us to the
reality in which we believe, or in other words, of
generating specifically Christian religious experience.[4] Just as being is not so much what is as what
happens, so Christian faith does not so much concern what we know about God as how he continues
to encounter us. Dewart thereby disengaged the
mission of Christianity from its message. The redemptive mission remains the same throughout the

ages, but the message assumes the linguistic and cultural forms that are proper to particular times and places. According to Dewart's notion of truth, what counts is how well conceptual expressions relate to man's ever more clear and conscious grasp of his religious experience in the context of the Church's redemptive mission. A dehellenization of dogma is called for, since many of our dogmas grew out of cultural experiences (that is, a consciousness of the world) which are foreign to us.

Dewart went further than merely insisting that content and expression are distinct, or that the event-character of revelation needs to be stressed. He seems to be saying that the content of a dogma— what a dogma means to affirm—is culturally conditioned. The meaning of a dogma represents the way religious consciousness at a particular time lived out the mission of Christ. Dewart did not think that his position was like that of the modernists, and I do not believe it is either. But it is hard to conceive the Christian mission as not requiring a Christian message, unless of course Dewart meant that the revelation of Christ and his redeeming action in our lives occur as an event rather than as a spoken message. In that case, the importance of a dogma derives from its relation to that event. Whether or not Christ had two wills, for instance, does not affect the saving mission of the Church.

However, Dewart did not state his case very well. He struggled with the common problem every theology of development faces, namely, how to reconcile identity and difference, permanence and change. Dewart was unable to explain how the self-same revelation continues to meet us even though the forms in which the mission of Christ is carried on and preached continue to change.

The Relationship between Gospel and Dogma

How is dogma related to revelation? Walter Kasper addressed this question by noting that dogma can have a claim on our faith only if dogma can be grounded in the gospel.[5]

On the surface, Kasper writes, gospel and dogma would appear to lie in some tension with each other. Gospel connotes Spirit, freedom, and life, while dogma suggests the institution, law, and fixed belief. After Luther, Protestant orthodoxy identified gospel and scripture, whereas Catholics tended to stress the unity of gospel and tradition and later on the unity between gospel and dogma. But the nineteenth century's interest in historical criticism brought the problem of dogmatic development to the fore. When the Church had to explain where its later dogmas came from, it centered on the relationship between scripture and tradition, not on gospel and dogma. For Kasper, this was an oversight.

Kasper recognized that a notion of truth and a theology of revelation are the two ideas that are essential for a theology of development; these two ideas must not be left mutually opposed. However, Kasper saw that the truth of dogma was usually discussed in terms of a very Western notion of truth, while the idea of truth operative in theologies of revelation has grown increasingly biblical. Failure to take account of this difference leads to a mistake:

> Up until now the history of dogma was really a piece of the cultural history of the West. It would be a novel kind of Judaism if the new nations were asked to learn to think the Western way before they could become Christian.[6]

There is a further problem. Not only is a more biblically founded notion of truth necessary to understand the nature of dogmatic truth, but every historical expression of the timeless event of revelation will be limited, including the scriptural statements. This fact creates a basic difficulty, namely,

> how the always other and neither historically nor dogmatically determinable gospel of the faithful truth of God maintains itself against the essentially deficient, historical testimony of the Church [7]

Kasper faced these problems by rethinking the nature of truth. The classical definition of truth as a conformity between the mind and reality (truth as correctness) was not rich enough to describe the truth of revelation. He looked both to the German philosopher Martin Heidegger and to scripture to present an enriched understanding of truth. In Heideggerian thought truth is conceived as an unveiling or revealing of being; for Heidegger truth is an event. And such a conception fits in well with a theology of revelation. Truth is not something to be identified with words or statements; truth happens when the words are spoken or read, and understood. Thus the truth of revelation cannot be equated with the words of scripture. Rather, the truth is hidden in the words and it appears when the words become meaningful to the hearer. Now that truth which reveals itself when the words of scripture are received in faith Kasper calls "the gospel." Jesus Christ unsurpassably unveiled and expressed through word and event God's saving designs; in this respect, Jesus is the gospel.

On the biblical side Kasper found two ways of defining truth. At the heart of biblical faith (and its world view) was Israel's experience of God as *the* faithful one; truth would have to be construed in terms of promise and fulfillment. The Israelites imprinted a sense of salvation history upon their existence as a people, an imprint that made their view of truth eschatological.[8] In the Gospel of John Kasper found that the Greek and Hebrew notions of truth were fused. A prophetic tone surrounds John's understanding of the Spirit as the one who will come and cause the disciples to remember all that Jesus told them. The testimony of the disciples and of the later Church about Jesus confirms that prophetic tone.

Unfortunately, the prophetic dimension of truth is easily forgotten in the life of the Church. But can Christ be preached without the prophetic dimension? Kasper writes: "The gospel originally was the power of Christ becoming public in the word of the proclamation in and over his Church."[9] Initially, gospel pertained to the work of the Spirit in the Church, not to written texts; the Spirit brings the gospel to life, and by that gospel the Church is judged. The Church therefore stands under the prophetic voice of the gospel.

One of the reasons why the eighteenth and nineteenth centuries took to the notion of tradition lay in the attempt to recapture a sense of the gospel as living in the Church. For Möhler, Kasper recalls, the gospel was "the complete doctrine of Christ, the living proclaimed kerygma before and along with the gospel which has become scriptural." The living gospel which is inscribed on the hearts of the faithful must accompany the gospel in its written form.[10]

Gospel accordingly appears as a larger category than dogma, though the two terms are not opposed as spirit and law; gospel is not anti-institutional or anti-dogmatic. A concept of dogma taken in the early sense of a rule of faith emerged in the primitive Church from a union of the concepts of law and truth (in its biblical meaning).[11] But truth always holds a certain priority over law.

What implications does Kasper see in all of this? First, the message of the gospel as located in the New Testament has been couched in language and representations with pronounced cultural roots. But the universality of the gospel indicates its independence from any one cultural or conceptual framework. Theological truth appears at the intersection of the timeless message and the here-and-now reception; it occurs in the tension between present and future hope, between letter and spirit, between the historical Jesus and the Christ of faith.[12]

Second, the truth of the gospel cannot be simply transposed into dogmatic formulas because gospel transcends every particular dogmatic or theological statement. It is based on the transcendence of God. Dogma can be defined as "the outcome of a historical experience of the Church in intimate contact with the gospel, an experience which becomes complete in Holy Scripture and in the community of the Church."[13]

Third, dogmatic statements are provisional. A final unveiling of divine truth must await until the end of time.

Fourth, theological truth is historical both with respect to its content and its unfolding. The content of that truth is the historical manifestation of God in Christ, his saving words and deeds. But the unfolding of that truth happens under historical circumstances and the Church must remain open to the future as well as to the prospect of further development.

So much for Walter Kasper. He has handled the epistemological side of the development question as well as anyone can. A great deal rests upon the Holy Spirit in his treatment. Since the gospel cannot be contained by the biblical words and the later dogmatic decrees, there is something charismatic about identifying the truth of the gospel. The Church must trust that when it discerns the gospel, the Spirit guarantees that the discernment will be genuine. That is a very Catholic position!

The Historicity of Dogma and Hermeneutics

A third way of tackling the problem of development is through hermeneutics. We have seen that some theologians distinguish meaning and expression and then draw attention to the historically conditioned nature of the expression. Avery Dulles, for example, points out the contextual nature of creedal statements, analyzes their positive meaning, and then establishes criteria for separating "the good grain of revelation from the chaff of historical relativity."[14] Piet Schoonenberg made the same distinction and then offered some hermeneutical principles for determining what past dogmatic statements mean for modern believers.[15] So also Gregory Baum.[16] Edward Schillebeeckx reaches the same point by explaining that a dogmatic truth maintains a double relationship: (1) a dogma is formulated against the background of a particular period in the life of the Church; (2) a dogma always looks toward the faith of the primitive Church. When we assent to a dogma, our faith is not directed to the formulation of the truth but (through the dogmatic truth) to God. A dogma can be defined as a "new formulation, relating to a particular situation, of the mystery of salvation experienced in the Church."[17] Therefore we rightly distinguish the relative from the unchanging aspects of dogma.

Each of these theologians is defending the legitimacy of contemporary efforts to render the meaning of past dogmas in a modern idiom. They are asking, what does this or that dogma actually mean? They presuppose the difference between revelation and scripture, the priority of gospel over dogma, and the fact (and the need) of tradition as the record of how revelation has been heard by past generations of believers. That record has a religious significance in its own right. Schoonenberg makes this point clear:

> The post-biblical tradition, including dogma, interprets Scripture but is itself interpreted by Scripture. Furthermore both tradition and Scripture must be understood in the light of the core of the Christian message, i.e., the gospel or kerygma . . . . I opt for the position . . . that Scripture contains substantially the entire Christian revelation and that the function of the post-biblical tradition is an explicative one.[18]

One could charge, however, that these accounts do not take history seriously enough. How is it that history affects the formulation of a dogmatic statement but not its basic meaning? After all, meaning has to be transmitted from one generation of believers to another, and those believers are historical creatures; whatever that permanent meaning is, it can only survive under the conditions of history. And that, of course, is what tradition is all about.

In a very fine piece of work, Thomas Ommen pursued this matter by appropriating the contemporary German discussion of hermeneutics, especially the contributions of Gerhard Ebeling and Hans-Georg Gadamer.[19] Ommen agreed with Ebeling's criticism of the meaning-expression or content-form distinction. Meaning cannot be neatly detached from modes of discourse, literary genres, the structure and function of symbolic language, and so forth. As Ebeling and Heidegger have shown, meaning is a language-event; meaning "happens"; meaning cannot be isolated from the words, sentences, and texts in which it resides. The insistence of Catholic theology upon the permanence of meaning in dogmatic statements was historically unfaithful (because historical continuity cannot always be demonstrated); Catholic theology relied far too heavily on authority to state definitively the meaning of texts and doctrines instead of facing the rigors of the hermeneutical task. But the principles of authority and tradition (as they have been generally understood and appealed to) do not settle the problem of development.

Suppose a theologian were attempting to reformulate a dogma. In that case he would first have to face the task of interpreting the dogmatic meaning. What would be involved? First, he acknowledges the historical nature of the world from which the dogma arose and the historical conditioning of his own world view. In the process of interpretation both of these worlds come together. Gadamer referred to this as the fusion of horizons, the horizon of the text and the horizon of the interpreter. If, for example, I were trying to understand the Gospel of

Mark, it would be impossible to get inside Mark's head; my only recourse is to try to understand his text with all the scholarly resources at my disposal and total understanding of Mark is impossible unless I come to share Mark's faith. Interpretation presupposes that the world of the text enjoys a certain independence or transcendence of meaning; or, in other words, that there is a story to be understood.

Second, besides what a writer meant to tell us, there are the words he used. We might read more into those words than he intended to say, but we cannot determine his intention if he is no longer around. Only his text and whatever supporting evidence scholarship may produce are available to us. The point is that language carries an excess of meaning over what is explicitly intended by an author's words. As soon as we hear or read something, we interpret the words. What do the words mean? What is implied? Are figures of speech being used? Any text that has been around for a long time will be interpreted over a wide variety of historical situations. Thus we can say that

> the full meaning of a dogma transcends the explicit intentions of a particular council or pope. A realm of meaning is carried along with the language of dogma which extends beyond the limits of the explicitly affirmed content of a given dogmatic statement.[20]

The relevance of a hermeneutical discussion to the problem of dogmatic development becomes

clear. Before considering the nature of development
in a strictly theological vein, one asks about language, meaning, and how interpretation takes place.
Development happens *because* meanings have been
received, understood, and transmitted. In other
words, if the problem posed by development asks
how permanence of meaning can be maintained
over time, the hermeneutical approach dissolves the
issue by answering that this way of phrasing the
problem betrays an unhistorical view of meaning
and truth.

According to Ommen, the meaning of a dogma
has to be examined in the light of a process of
transmission which stretches back to scripture itself. Since all texts characteristically enjoy an
openness toward further interpretation, dogmatic
meanings which lie along the trajectory of a
scriptural text as it arches into the future have to be
interpreted in the light of scripture:

> Dogma is properly interpreted in the light of
> Scripture, for it represents the future of biblical
> texts themselves. The post-biblical tradition,
> including dogma, constitutes the ongoing pro-
> cess of the interpretation of scriptural texts.[21]

Later interpretation of dogmatic meaning will
never amount simply to repeating the meanings contained in scripture. Rather, as Ommen points out,
the scriptural text opens up an area of experience
that was not entirely actualized in apostolic times.
This area widens a little further each time the horizons of text and interpreter merge anew.

Hermeneutical analysis marks a genuine contribution to the problem of dogmatic development. It acknowledges the historical moment in the formulation *and* the meaning of a dogmatic truth, and situates dogma along the historical path of the proclamation, reception, and transmission of scripture. The key is to view dogma as emerging from the fusion of two worlds, the world of apostolic experience and faith, and the world of any given generation of believers. This approach succeeds very well in relating scripture and tradition. It admits with Newman that the process of development indeed manifests a certain growth and expansion of the apostolic message, and it explains with the main line theologians how later development is continuous with the deposit of revelation.

The Future of Dogma

With the personalist theology of revelation featured in Vatican II, the Church also recognized that in the economy of salvation there exists a hierarchy of truths which relate at various levels to the foundation of Christian faith (see the "Decree on Ecumenism," #11). This admission comes as a corollary to the view that there are degrees of incorporation into the mystery of the Church ("Dogmatic Constitution on the Church," #14-16). In short, the Council's theology of the Church carries implications for dogmatic theology. The direction of a renewed Church is toward the personal center of its life, namely, Jesus Christ. Catholic faith is built upon the basic unity and simplicity which are the person and work of Jesus. Although the Church proposes many dogmas to be believed, the result ought not to be a scattering of faith but a centering. Just as there are degrees of communion in the Church (all heading toward a fullness and simplicity of life), so also the dogmatic truths of faith (which comprise an order of importance) converge upon the unity and simplicity of the object of faith. The process of development will not be of service to the Church unless it moves in the direction of greater simplicity, making it possible for believers to attend more closely to the center of their new life. For that reason, Dulles distinguishes primary and secondary truths of faith. While not discounting the secondary truths, he makes a pastoral bid for respecting the sensitivities of the people to whom we preach today:

> The principle of economy would require us to be slow to insist upon secondary points which our hearers are not yet prepared to accept. Respecting the free and personal character of the assent of faith, we ought not to insist that individual believers should see everything from the beginning or that they should assent to doctrines in which they can as yet find no meaning, relevance, or credibility. Patience is demanded to give people time to grow into the fullness of the truth.[22]

This kind of attitude will come very hard to those who insist that because something is true, it makes no difference whether it is of primary or secondary importance. And once a dogma is added to the confession of faith, it must remain there for all time! In the organic model of development there is a danger of making the process of development irreversible in the direction of a multiplicity of dogmas. Yet the dynamics of faith steer toward greater unity and simplicity.

Gerald O'Collins examined the concept of dogma in detail and concluded that the word is not serviceable; it should be dropped. First, by proposing dogmas for belief, we obscure the fact that the object of faith is not the dogma but God. Second, the term "dogma" has been too widely applied (it includes too many beliefs, some of which are less important than others); the term is also of quite recent usage as a technical theological expression. Third, the language of a dogmatic definition is analogous and sometimes symbolic. O'Collins believes that there is no single meaning of a particular dogma; dogmas are intrinsically open to a certain pluralism of meaning. Fourth, dogmas carry different degrees of authority. Some arose from local church synods, some from Church councils, some from the popes. Some deal with insignificant points while others bear directly on salvation. Fifth, dogmatic orthodoxy is no substitute for right living. The fierceness with which dogmas have been defended often surpassed the zeal spent on inciting believers to holiness of life. Only a truth that is lived can be sanctifying. Sixth, no dogma can rise to the importance of inspired scripture, and since Vatican II the Church has invited believers more and more to meditate on, study, and appreciate the sacred writings. For all these reasons, dogma appears too unwieldy a term to serve the pastoral mission of the Church.[23] But the limitations of the term do not mean that Christian faith becomes a mission without a message. O'Collins has simply called for a more appropriate manner of expressing that message while we are engaged in the mission of making people holy.

Footnotes to Chapter 3

1. Leslie Dewart, *The Future of Belief* (New York, 1966). On reactions to Dewart see *The Future of Belief Debate*, ed. Gregory Baum (New York, 1967). For Lonergan's very critical review, see "The Dehellenization of Dogma" in *A Second Collection*.
2. Dewart, *The Future of Belief*, p. 92.
3. Ibid., p. 114.
4. Ibid., pp. 112-13.
5. The main work Kasper has written on the subject is *Dogma unter dem Wort Gottes* (Mainz, 1965); we shall cite this as *Dogma*.
6. Kasper, "The Relationship between Gospel and Dogma: An Historical Approach" in *Man as Man and Believer* (New York, 1967 [*Concilium*, vol. 21]), p. 165.
7. *Dogma*, p. 45.
8. *Dogma*, p. 78.
9. *Dogma*, p. 84.
10. *Dogma*, pp. 90-91.
11. Cf. "The Relationship between Gospel and Dogma," p. 155.
12. *Dogma*, pp. 100-101.
13. *Dogma*, pp. 139-42.
14. Avery Dulles, *The Survival of Dogma*, pp. 168-182. See also Raymond J. Devettere, "Progress and Pluralism in Theology," *Theological Studies* 35 (1974), 441-466.

15. Piet Schoonenberg, S.J., "Historicity and the Interpretation of Dogma," *Theology Digest* 18 (1970), 132-143.

16. Gregory Baum, *Faith and Doctrine: A Contemporary View* (New York, 1969), pp. 101ff.

17. Edward Schillebeeckx, O.P., *Concept of Truth and Theological Renewal* (London, 1968), p. 24.

18. Schoonenberg, art. cit., pp. 136, 137.

19. Thomas B. Ommen, *The Hermeneutic of Dogma* (Missoula, 1975).

20. Ibid., p. 195.

21. Ibid., pp. 200-201.

22. Avery Dulles, S.J., *The Resilient Church* (New York, 1977), p. 57.

23. Gerald O'Collins, S.J., *The Case Against Dogma* (New York, 1974).

4
The Unfinished Business

A number of questions become relevant to a discussion of dogmatic development. An adequate theology of development will have to address these issues.

One of the thrusts behind the present philosophical picture is process thought. In his great book *Process and Reality,* A. N. Whitehead took issue with classical Western metaphysics and particularly with the direction taken by modern philosophy since Descartes. Whitehead argued that reality would be better understood in terms of the philosophical category of relation rather than substance. The prevailing philosophical viewpoint, especially in Catholic circles, had descended from Aristotle. Aristotle had distinguished substance and accident, and substance referred to the important, essential, basic principle of things. Such a viewpoint translated into a rather static conception of being, and consequently, of truth. Classical thought realized that things change, of course; but change could be either accidental or substantial. Substantial change involved a corruption of what something essentially is. On the theological side of this view, a dogmatic truth could change accidentally (its language and expression), but never radically. Otherwise you would have a different meaning (substance) altogether. In the limiting case, God himself had to be timeless and immutable.

The problem with the classicist perspective, however, was its inability to grasp the nature of change and what history is. History is not the temporal march of timeless, unchanging substances or truths couched in ephemeral modes of dress. Historical process is slightly more complex than that. Reality is in process; all things exist in a network of relations such that ultimately nothing in the universe stands totally unrelated to everything else. When one thing changes, everything else is somehow affected, however minimally. Reality is in flux. By concentrating on the essence or basic features of things, the classicist perspective lifted those things from the network of relationships into an abstract scheme where essences remained fixed and immutable. God therefore does not have a *real* relation to the world because, being immutable, he cannot be affected by an historically processive universe.

From this perspective, for example, one theologizes about salvation without attending to how individual Christians concretely experience and manifest God's saving grace. But salvation and redemption are not a couple of abstract notions, although the words tend to conjure up a very high abstraction. They designate what is happening to believers in the concrete circumstances of their daily lives.

Salvation history is quite concrete. The Bible reveals the experience of a people materially (not just mentally) encountering God in the events of their lives and in the history of their nation. The God of scripture, as Abraham Heschel suggests, or the God of Christian experience, as David Tracy insists, has a real relation to the world.[1]

Truth As Event

Although it definitely possesses conceptual content, revelation is not comparable to an idea, as Newman put it, because revelation is more than a set of propositions about God. The non-propositional or event character of revelation squares far more easily with a process view of reality than with a static one. The process view takes seriously the concrete, here-and-now occurrence of God's encountering us. Revealed truth, therefore, *happens*. Salvation is based upon two happenings, namely, the dying and rising of Jesus. The teaching of Jesus was given to us, not that we should merely be better informed about God, but that we should repent and follow his Son. Repenting (or change of heart) and following are events.

It is helpful to distinguish truth in its primary and secondary modes. Primarily, truth is an event.[2]

In a faith context we could say that God's saving truth happened through his saving deeds. In general we could say that truth is the revealing or "coming-to-presence" of being. Reality shows itself as meaningful; meaning is a language event which is accomplished in the process of understanding, interpreting, or speaking. Secondarily, then, truth is articulated in sentences and verbal statements. Meaning is resident in words, but actually occurs in the act of understanding. A statement is true by virtue of its relation to an event. For example, a dogma is termed a truth of faith. But the importance of a dogma derives from its relation to what God has done; a dogma states something pertaining to our salvation. The dogmatic statement (the manner of dress) is thus derivatively true.

With this way of thinking, the notion of truth becomes rich indeed. Truth lives; it transforms and sanctifies. To identify truth with the adequacy of our ideas and not with the events of God's redeeming love impoverishes the meaning of dogma. If dogma only reflected information about God, then Christ might be represented as a gnostic revealer of divine secrets and not as the concrete sacrament of the Father's grace. Dogmas therefore are supposed to translate the truth of revelation into language.

The classical mind defined truth as a conformity between the mind and reality. Truth was embodied in propositions. But propositions tend to be rather lifeless; they can be repeated countless times as definitive, fixed expressions of what is so. Being or reality comes across as timeless and unchanging as the statements we use to describe it. Instead of letting the mind conform itself with reality, the mind exerts its own control and makes reality conform to the restrictions of our limited way of knowing. That, of course, was the problem which Immanuel Kant identified.

Now the difficulty is not so great when the language used is obviously symbolic, because symbolic language invites openness, interpretation, and development. But technical language attempts to fix meanings precisely. While words can, of course, be used to define our meaning, we make a mistake if we feel that because of our definitions, reality has been summed up, defined, and packaged. Religious language is no exception. God is slightly larger than our ideas about him. Ideas are measured against what God reveals; God is not measured by the way we come to think about him.

All this probably seems extremely obvious. But I make these points because they help to explain why theologians are rethinking what dogma is all about. The central issue is not that ideas develop and unfold (which they do); the issue is that *we* are alive, that *we* develop because of the interpenetration of new experiences and our beliefs. To formulate the problem of dogmatic development in terms of expression and content does not do enough justice, I think, to the organic, open, processive character of the universe. In other words, dogmatic development is not primarily an epistemological matter; it is an ontological one. And consequently, the actual problem which theologians have been facing is that of reconciling immutability and historical process.

Dogmatic language is somewhat bewitching. It purports to be timeless; it implicitly claims that revelation is unchanging, immutable. But that is only half the story. Does a theologian really do justice to the nature of reality if he takes a non-propositional and historical approach to revelation, and a propositional view of truth? Truth too is non-propositional in its primary mode. In addition, however, I want to suggest that the term "immutable" is misleading in a discussion where the principle point is raised because we are historical creatures.

How Does Revelation Take Place?

The answer to this question is not complicated, although it involves a number of things. First, to put the matter negatively, revelation is not identical with the history of biblical interpretation. Such a conclusion may perhaps have been drawn on the basis of Thomas Ommen's contribution, or indeed from the hermeneutical approach generally. Nor is it accurate to say that revelation is actualized through interpretation of the gospel texts. Revelation is neither hermeneutics nor exegesis. Revelation happens, that is, God meets us through scripture as a window frames the daylight. Its accent falls on the revealing action of God through inspiration, devotion, prayer, etc., which scripture occasions. That action also occurs in liturgy, in sacramental celebration, through homilies and shared prayer.

In his book *Ecclesial Man* (Philadelphia, 1975), Edward Farley considered from a phenomenological perspective how the Christian message is ecclesially mediated. There are a number of basic, positive facts which make up the identity of the Christian community. We shall always be committed to those facts if we are to remain Christian. Redemption, which Farley describes as overcoming alienated existence, takes place in the context of the Church. Redemptive activity is framed by the liturgical forms, styles of prayer, sacred texts, etc., that the community has adopted. The historical events concerning Jesus Christ which are sedimented in the life and corporate memory of the Church persist in the day to day faith of the community. These concrete forms of faith "structure" the way redemption happens and make it possible for us to identify that event as Christian.

Revelation, therefore, happens concretely through the religious structures of Christian faith. Instead of using the word "immutable" with its unhistorical overtone, Farley speaks of the "positive" historical events which continue to shape the way revelation and redemption occur.

Let me offer an example. The dogma of the Trinity states conceptually the Christian understanding of God, and that understanding is a major element in marking the distinctiveness of Christian faith. Yet fundamentally the Trinity is not a great idea. It represents the way God acts and gives himself to us. Thus we speak of his creative action (and providential guidance of the world), his redeeming action, and his sanctifying action. The dogma is based on these events; each of the divine Persons *does* something. The dogma articulates our understanding of God; yet even more it reflects the manner in which God has shared himself. By attending to the creedal statement, the believer becomes open to the possibility of the Christian experience of God. The dogma protects the integrity of that experience because it keeps the Church committed to its past, that is, to the faith experience of the apostolic Church.

This is what Lonergan was getting at when he wrote about the permanence of dogmatic meaning. I wonder, though, if that permanence actually rests upon the immutability of God, as Vatican I maintained. Perhaps it is wiser to keep the issue more sociological: the Church as an historical community preserves its identity through the way it structures its day to day existence, especially through scripture, preaching, and sacrament. Those structures embrace through historical remembrance the original redemptive events, and they mediate the revelation of God to the present.

"Positivity" makes more sense than "immutability" to describe how the same revelation continues to occur, since the Church's intent is not so much to settle whether God changes as to declare that our present encounter with him is historically continuous with the experience of the apostles.

Furthermore, historical process will require that revelation address later generations within their particular frameworks. The manner in which those believers articulate their experience of God may well differ from the expression of a previous age.

But they remain nonetheless committed to the memory and presence of Jesus Christ, and to the religious forms which preserve that memory and structure the possibility of his presence. Whether or not all our dogmas indeed do this adequately is open to discussion. To what degree the past formulas interfere with revelation's happening today is a current issue in catechetics. This concern is as alive for Leslie Dewart and Hans Küng as it is for Avery Dulles, Karl Rahner, and Paul VI.

Tradition: The Historical Transmission of Apostolic Faith

We ought also to remark that historical continuity bears primarily upon apostolic faith, not on ecclesiastical structures or dogmas. One age did not have defective faith because it had not confessed the dogma of a later time or lived with the same kind of church order. The fullness of saving truth, as we have seen, is not to be equated with verbal statements about that truth. Redemption is accomplished as the transforming events in a person's life. That is why Dulles and the theologians of Vatican II could speak of a hierarchy of doctrines, for the proclamation of the death and resurrection of Jesus, and the saving action of the Father, Son, and Spirit, are absolutely central to Christian faith. The faith-response to such good news is justifying; this is the faith "come down to us from the apostles." All other doctrines are rooted in these.

I would like to register some misgivings about the "global experience" idea in Rahner and Walgrave (expanding upon Newman) as a way of explaining how the fullness of faith is transmitted. Herbert Hammans wrote about the apostles:

> There are many things of which they [the apostles] had no explicit knowledge; yet, in a sense, they knew all inasmuch as they embraced the whole reality of God's saving act and lived spiritually in this reality. And because they "knew" it in a fulfilled manner, the Church's awareness of the faith in a later age is not superior to the simple awareness of the apostles.[3]

But where does such an experience reside? How is it transmitted? To talk about a pre-conceptual experience of the apostles is one thing; to explain how it could possibly be transmitted is another. With Anthony Stephenson one would be forced to conclude: "For hypothetical revealed but not transmitted knowledge the only place known to theological epistemology is the broader class of the unrevealed."[3]

What needs to be said is that the process of transmission is as concrete, positive, and historical as the occurrence of revelation itself. Scripture was collected through a process of transmission and therefore remains the product of tradition. Scripture is a function of revelation. Tradition is not a font of revelation (another "source" alongside scripture), for revelation does not consist of a body of propositions. Tradition includes the process of transmitting the faith. Essentially ecclesial, tradition is the lived, ongoing experience of faith as mediated by scripture, sacrament, communal discernment, lifestyle, and so forth. The global experience sounds too distant and timeless, like an idea out of Plato's noetic heaven. The intention behind the global experience idea is to explain how one receives a comprehensive sense for what Christianity is by one's active membership in the daily life of the community with its worship, its preaching, and its faith.

In short, there is no such thing as an a-historical communication of experience; communication takes place in a concrete social matrix. To put the matter another way, the development of dogma does not prescind from a sociology of knowledge. The Holy Spirit guarantees that revelation is spoken to every new generation. The meaning of revelation may become obscured by the infidelity or deafness of an age, but the Spirit assures us that within the community there will always exist *the possibility* of hearing God's voice in the concrete structures of its religious life.

Where Do New Dogmas Come From?

Some theologians feel that the Church's dogmas can be located at least seminally in scripture. In fact, those who settle the development problem by appealing to the content-expression distinction are logically committed to this view. Since some rule of faith had to be operative in the primitive tradition to guide the composition and eventual collecting of the New Testament writings, the New Testament canon itself could be regarded as an expression of the essential content of Christian faith. On this showing, the New Testament, expressing the core of Christian belief, becomes the basis for further doctrinal elaboration. Thus Rudolf Bultmann wrote: "All that develops is simply our way of talking about revelation."[4] In his recent book *Blessed Rage for Order*, David Tracy sized up the issue in terms of the need to correlate Christian texts and common human experience. This means that dogmatic development and revelation occur in the conjunction of scripture and present day cultural experience, like the horizon fusion of the hermeneutical approach. Anthony Stephenson, who sharply criticized Newman, thought that the phrase "development of dogma" was a theological disaster and maintained that "the full Christological and Trinitarian doctrine is really, objectively, and unquestionably contained in Scripture."[5]

There are obvious advantages to locating all the later dogmas in scripture. Principally, this strategy enables one to defend the continuity of later faith with the primitive Church. But it seems to me that it entails some overriding weaknesses. For one thing, we would be hard pressed to uncover the Marian dogmas in scripture without resorting to some theological sleight of hand. The history of dogma includes many a gap if you look only to the Bible. That is the reason why the Church appealed to tradition as another "source" of revelation. Yet more critically, attempting to locate dogmas in scripture tends to make revelation propositional. It makes Nicea and Chalcedon, for example, simply other ways of stating what is already recorded in scripture. But how clearly and unambiguously?

Dogma is not a function of scripture; it is a function of revelation. As Kasper argued, dogma relates to gospel. Revelation is non-propositional in its primary mode. Further, if the later dogmas only restate what scripture has recorded, then why the bother? Why not side with the Greek-speaking Fathers against Athanasius and reject *homoouslos* as non-scriptural and therefore unnecessary? To make later dogmas mere reformulations of scripture, I think, is to collapse the later tradition by making history an object lesson in what happens when one misinterprets scripture. It runs the risk of a Catholic fundamentalism and fails to appreciate the distinctive way in which later generations heard God's revelation as addressed to them and responded to it.

Let me offer an opinion that the Church would be unable to declare a dogma unless it was capable of experiencing and understanding the gospel anew. Revelation must be conceived as an ongoing event in the life of the Church; the Church lives out of its ongoing experience of the revelation given in Christ. If tradition means the lived interpretation of the gospel, then dogma is part of tradition and represents an articulation of how God has revealed himself. We ought not to dismiss dogmas (even granting the fact that they occupy a hierarchy of importance) because they are indications of how past generations heard and interpreted God's address to them. Such, I think, is the only way to overcome the scandal of history. Christianity is more than an ancient faith. It is born anew, as it were, from age to age, as the gospel is proclaimed and received afresh. Dogmas bear witness to that fact.

An Ambiguity with the Word "Development"

Using the phrase *"development* of dogma" invites a possible misunderstanding. Development implies an ordered growth, such as we observe in the maturation of a seed or in the advance of natural science. The development of theology reveals how much we have grown in understanding the faith. If we are not to devalue the role of intelligence in discovering the truth, then we have to recognize in the development of theology an important component in the way God's address reaches any given age. Theology too serves to make us attend to what the Lord is saying to us. Sometimes, by the "development of dogma" one is actually signifying the development of theology.

Yet the development of dogma should not be automatically equated with the development of theological science. Logic plays a bigger part in the growth of scientific understanding than in dogmatic development. For, as Lonergan and Rahner put it, the intelligibility of dogmatic development is chiefly the intelligibility of historical process. Besides, revelation does not develop; only the concrete modes in which revelation is mediated can be said to develop.

Scripture is a primary instance of development.

The gospels, for example, manifest both a diversity of theological perspective and the early Church's growing reflection on the mystery of Christ. Liturgical forms develop. Styles of prayer, rules of faith, and expressions of belief develop. Church order develops. Yet these structures of ecclesial existence are not coincident with revelation. Through them, as we noted, historical faith is transmitted. This is what I take to be the reasoning behind distinguishing the expression and content of a dogma: expression mediates content. But I tend to agree with Kasper that the theological issue here is not changeable expression and immutable content. Rather, the issue is the relation between dogma and gospel. Dogma reflects the way a particular generation grasped the significance of the gospel, an expression of the way God revealed himself to that age. In listening to our tradition, we have to pay attention to the way God has spoken to our ancestors, if we are to learn what sort of people we are. His voice in history utters what we too need to hear.

Footnotes to Chapter 4

1. See Heschel's book *The Prophets* (New York, 1962), and Tracy's *Blessed Rage for Order: The New Pluralism in Theology* (New York, 1975), pp. 172-187.

2. This is a Heideggerian formulation. I have never heard of something on Heidegger for the non-specialist, but a good book on Heidegger's notion of truth is W. B. Macomber, *The Anatomy of Disillusion* (Evanston, Ill., 1967).

3. Herbert Hammans, "Recent Catholic Views on the Development of Dogma," in *Man as Man and Believer*

(Concilium, vol. 21; New York, 1967), pp. 116-17.

4. Rudolf Bultmann, *Existence and Faith* (New York, 1960), p. 89.

5. Anthony A. Stephenson, S.J., "The Development and Immutability of Christian Doctrine," *Theological Studies* 19 (1958), p. 511.

Appendix:
A Word about Heresy

I mentioned in the Preface that a word or two ought to be said about heresy. The word "heresy" was perhaps overused in the past by people who did not understand that a legitimate theological pluralism could exist within the parameters of orthodox faith. To be sure, the Church has evidenced a real pluralism in accepting different approaches to spirituality and different schools of theology. But a Church that was predominantly Western and committed for the most part to the ideal of theological science exemplified by St. Thomas Aquinas had little idea of the wider dimensions of pluralism. That there can be a variety of perspectives on the gospel, arising from non-Western thought-forms and linguistic expressions, and the revolution triggered by a better technical grasp of scripture—these have contributed greatly to the Church's positive reassessment of pluralism. This situation obviously calls for a great deal of caution before applying the label "heretic" to someone, because the label implies an accusation of bad faith based on a person's stubbornness and intransigence:

> According to the classical rules, the fact of one's professing "heresy" can only be definitively established if the accused theologian has demonstrated "obstinacy," that is, if he closes himself off from all discussion meant to clarify an opinion contrary to the faith and, in effect, refuses the dialogue [with the magisterium and theologians from various schools]. The fact of heresy can be established only after all the rules of the hermeneutics of dogmas and all the theological qualifications have been applied. In this way, even in decisions which cannot be avoided, the true "ethos" of the dialogue-procedure can be preserved.[1]

Heresy, however, does not always have to imply bad faith. The development of classical christology and trinitarian theology reads like a problem that had gone out of control. Solutions were advanced, sometimes very inadequately, to explain the unity of the Father and Son, then their distinction, then their relationship to the Holy Spirit, then the relation of the divine Logos to the human Christ, and so on. One question invited another, and all of them had to be hammered out against the ambiguities of scripture. For example, the Arians were unable to understand why Jesus was not a creature (albeit a most perfect creature). If there were two things in God (Father and Son), then the divine substance would be divided and the unity of God would be fractured. Many of the eastern bishops during the early fourth century had been influenced by Origen. They found it difficult to conceive how "of the same stuff" *(homoousios)* safeguarded the apostolic faith. For, while rejecting the Arians' claim that Christ was not co-equal and co-eternal with God, neither would they agree that there was an identity of substance between Father and Son; that smacked of Sabellianism, a view which collapsed the distinction between Father and Son. Given their background, a non-Sabellian interpretation of *homoousios* was hardly possible. They could not get a handle on their philosophical assumptions. Subsequent theology would be riddled with false starts, many of them quite earnest, before the "one substance, three persons" formula of Chalcedon appeared.

The point of this little bit of history is to illustrate that in the often heated, theologically uncertain, and culturally diverse atmosphere of the third, fourth, and fifth centuries, many thinkers subscribed to and defended positions which eventually proved unorthodox. The fact that the history of the time was largely recorded by orthodox authors, who took a dim view of their religious opponents, skewed later judgment unfairly.

Lonergan made a very helpful observation about that period when he distinguished two kinds of development that were going on.[2] First, there was the development of trinitarian and christologi-

cal doctrine. Second, there was the development of
the very notion of dogma, that is, a reflective attempt to control the meaning of the gospels by attending to them as *true*. Something is called "true"
with respect to a horizon of meanings. Now, the
technical control of meaning depends upon a somewhat technical grasp of what human knowledge and
metaphysics are all about. But the lack of technical
mastery over one's concepts and assumptions does
not imply bad faith. Bad faith can only be proved by
a failure in charity. The eastern Fathers were not
trying to be contrary by registering their dismay
with the term *homoousios*. But the Arians had used
the term too. And their pastoral instinct led some of
them to prefer the ambiguity of scripture over the
precedent-setting introduction of a non-scriptural
word into the Church's ordinary catechesis.

Heresy As Evil

The evil of heresy appears on two related
fronts. First, heresy can harm the truth by its rejection or simply by its misapprehension of what is so.
Second, heresy injures the unity of the Church because it breaks down the communion of hearts and
minds. If truth is meant to serve the unity and holiness of the Church, then disunity emerges as the
real malice of heresy. Today, as Karl Rahner sug-
gested, heresy may have assumed the shape of
atheism and materialism—shapes all the more sinis-
ter because they are so fluid and pervasive, because
they disembowel the gospel's radical claim on
Christian life.

Of course, there are still voices which deny the divinity of Christ, and these must be sharply divided from theologians who are struggling to determine in a contemporary idiom what the divinity of Christ means. But is the divinity of Christ being attacked today from theological quarters? Rather, isn't the assault arising from those who have so divorced faith and justice that what Christ is has no bearing on the way they view the social order? After all, if men and women have become partakers of the divine nature because of grace, what shall we say of those Christians who fail to see the divinity of Christ in their fellow men? The rights and dignity of human beings cannot be abridged without denying an important feature of the dogma about Christ's divinity. The consequence of this lived denial upon the Church is extremely grave, because this heresy paves the way for revolution and the disintegration of communion. And this is what liberation theology means by its insistence that orthodoxy and orthopraxis (right living) cannot be separated.

But God brings good even out of evil, for those who love him. Heresy has its salutary side. Since it distorts the gospel in some way, heresy constrains the Church to listen more attentively to the whole of the gospel. As a result, divine revelation is received with a new freshness by another generation of believers.

Again, the classical heresies (Adoptionism, Arianism, Pelagianism, etc.) usually functioned dialectically. A denial of some doctrine or a mistaken understanding became the occasion of new theological reflection and synthesis. Leon Cristiani writes: "but there has always been an insistence on the good which can come from the great evil of heresy, for every heresy has been the occasion of progress in understanding of the faith, and of a strengthening of unity within the Church."[3]

An Evil Which Besets Dogma

Revelation is God's free, gracious act. Revelation cannot be forced; it "comes"; and we, like the young Samuel, wait for the Lord to speak. Revelation is not neatly processed and packaged, whether in scriptural phrases or dogmatic formulas. The meaning of those words has to be retrieved under grace; they must be listened to in faith.

Dogmas are finite statements. Divine truths, yes, but laid in human words and concepts. Their finiteness should be a constant reminder that no statement or collection of statements will ever exhaust the infinite richness of divine truth. There are things about God we do not know, and, so far as our salvation is concerned, we do not need to know. Neither a dogma, nor a creed, nor a set of inspired writings contains the fullness of revelation; rather, they point to that fullness (what God does want us to have, what we do need to know) through the intrinsic limitation of human words, images, concepts, and symbols.

But suppose the finiteness of dogmatic statements is forgotten? Suppose the formulas are elevated to a timelessness beyond the historicity that touches all things human, even the most revered religious expressions? In that case, I suggest, the statements become empty forms; they would have presumed the prerogatives of transcendence. We believe that the Holy Spirit enables scripture to mediate the presence of God, and that without the Spirit scripture degenerates into a naive fundamentalism. In the same way, dogma which is proposed and confessed without the Spirit falls into dogmatism. In other words, dogma will obscure the very thing it was meant to confess when the limits of dogma are forgotten. In such a case, dogma would become heresy! Perhaps not in the villainous manner which we associate with the polemics of ancient heresies, but in the manner of mediating error instead of truth.

The fact is that we do not know everything about God. The fact is that we do not dictate the word of God; we are under it. Divine truth is not served by anything less than the simple humility which acknowledges revelation as God's free, totally gracious act.

Perhaps heresy and error ought to be distinguished. Not every mistake assumes the proportions of heresy, just as many bright ideas do not automatically become dogmas. Only when the mistake starts to break apart the unity of the Church should we be talking about heresy. If every error were an incipient heresy, then it would stand to reason that the Church will forever harbor some closet heretics. After all, the error that crops up because the actual meaning of a dogma is forgotten or because its limitations are overlooked will be perennial. Human beings forget. When they further forget their proneness to being forgetful, then indeed they mistake the light for darkness, truth for error. That is why, I suppose, God raises up prophets and teachers in the Church—to remind us that we are receivers of divine truth, not the owners. It is, of course, a humbling experience to be informed of one's error, and to realize that in this life we remain susceptible to a certain degree of blindness. Yet such realization is itself a moment of grace. Forgetting is not all that terrible if it brings about a deeper appreciation of the truth.

Heresy and the Development of Dogma

Centuries ago, St. Hilary of Poitiers wrote:

The errors of heretics and blasphemers force us to deal with unlawful matters, to scale perilous heights, to speak unutterable words, to trespass on forbidden ground. Faith ought in silence to fulfill the commandments, worshiping the Father, reverencing with him the Son, abounding in the Holy Spirit, but we must strain the poor resources of our language to express thoughts too great for words in daring to embody in human terms truths which ought to be hidden in the silent veneration of the heart.[4]

Heresy has played a very exciting role in dogmatic development, for dogmas were often defined in reaction to it. Heresy therefore influenced the course of historical development considerably. But which positions were heterodox and which ones would emerge as Catholic was not always too clear. In fact, positions not initially regarded as heretical were often denounced only after their sponsors had died. Origen was a case in point.

The reasons why a given heresy arose vary from case to case. Many factors—geographical, social, political, cultural, philosophical—come into play. Questions that the evangelists never faced were addressed to succeeding centuries, and the attempt to answer them easily led to mistakes and oversights. The classical heresies of the ancient christological and trinitarian controversies were characteristic of a Church attempting to understand and clarify its faith. In the thirteenth century the ideal of evangelical poverty was lived and canonized in the example of St. Francis, but persecuted and condemned less than a century later; what was spiritual reform for Innocent III became doctrinal error for John XXII.[5] Many a protestant might have been reconciled with Rome had the pope granted the reformers' request for vernacular in the liturgy and communion under both kinds. In this particular case, a bad practice had become so institutionalized that even Trent forgot how historical an entity the Church was. There were good reasons why many reformers rejected sacraments and championed scripture, or why Vatican II's Declaration on Religious Liberty could not have been written by Boniface VIII. A pope who views himself as a temporal ruler will react differently to heresy from a pope who knows that he is a bishop and a spiritual leader. St. Paul could express his thinking about the Eucharist without the philosophical understanding of substance, but he would have been unable to think about the Eucharist apart from the meaning of the Church. For men like Paul, Cyprian, and Augustine, orthodoxy was to be determined through the reality and desire for church unity. The reformers, on the other hand, drove the Church unwittingly to separate eucharist and church—at least for purposes of dogmatic definition. An excessive concentration on what is true in substantial and ontological terms, coupled with the principle of *ex opere operato,* lends itself to forgetting the fact that the presence of Christ is rather meaningless without faith in the believer's heart. Protestantism combatted one error by inviting another, for one cannot have an historical religion without tradition, and justifying faith should lead in the direction of greater unity, not lesser.

Sometimes in the dialectic between error and insight, bad faith has been involved, as when charity evaporated around power plays, lies, and treachery. At other times positions were adopted whose inherent weakness or outright error could not be immediately detected. What is remarkable, however, is that often the Church did not know where the truth actually lay. The truth of the gospel emerged only slowly into the light of clarity. Sometimes the air was heavy with obscurity and uncertainty; it was cleared through a process of reflection and discernment, through listening to the tradition and consulting revered authorities, by examining the faith as embodied in liturgical worship, through the intellectual struggles of gifted theologians, and so on.

A dogmatically ambiguous situation is not heretical. It merely demonstrates how much the Church needs to attune itself to hearing the gospel, to discerning the voice of the living Lord in the signs of the times. I think attunement is a good word to express the Church's dependence on the gospel. A period of dogmatic ambiguity serves to remind the Church of that dependent relation. If one views dogmatic truth as a good, as the coming-to-expression of revelation here and now, then it would appear that ambiguity is not always a bad thing. As a result of the ambiguity, the word of God is better heard and understood. What showed itself as an evil became an opportunity for the Church to attune itself again to God's word.

The enunciation of a dogma, however, is only one way of responding to error. Heresy not only contributed to the development of dogma; it also contributed to the development of spirituality, to liturgical and structural reforms. And by "heresy" I do not mean just the rejection of an orthodox position. People reject positions for a reason. Sometimes the reason was a mistaken philosophical assumption; sometimes it was disappointment over the Church's sinfulness; sometimes it stemmed from the conviction that more than one way existed for expressing the Christian faith. Truth has to live and sanctify people, if it is to be saving truth. When truth no longer lives, then its real claim is hidden, obscured, concealed from view. The Catholic who does not live his faith does as much harm to the Church as the heretic outside, as Augustine said. Instead of living the truth, one lives a lie; and that is heresy too. Saints like John of the Cross and Teresa of Avila fought against heresy of that sort. The Second Vatican Council, which I take to be the Church's authentic response to the Protestant reformers, was centuries in coming; it represented the Church finally facing modernity, theological pluralism and cultural diversity. Its accent upon interior renewal, its endorsement of scripture and biblical perspectives, its inaugurating liturgical reform, its defense of religious freedom—not to mention its esteem for the holiness and gifts of laypeople—all these things took a while in coming, but they represent truly orthodox responses to many errors, oversights, and personal and corporate sins.

Heresy As Not Listening

Perhaps heresy ought only to designate the unwillingness to listen, to be open. Mistakes can be corrected with education, openness, and patience. But a basic closure to God's word, manifested by obstinacy, deceit, and intolerance can only be corrected by conversion. The struggle to obtain clarity does not destroy communion, but smugness will do it every time. Just as dogma arises from the readiness to hear God's revelation and primarily represents a disclosure of divine truth (and, secondarily, the linguistic presentation of that truth); so, I think, heresy comes from a deep closedness to revelation and symbolizes a concealment of divine truth (which is, secondarily, expressed by erroneous beliefs and self-absorbed lifestyles).

In the history of dogma, one is not always dealing with this kind of heresy. But when it does appear, you must view it as one facet of the problem of evil. Ultimately, like dogmatic development, heresy is not merely a matter of wrong thinking; it is ontological and, indeed, theological.

"Whatever happened to heresy?" Well, if one means why doesn't the Church issue more anathemas, perhaps it is because we have learned that revelation is both larger and simpler than our scriptural, liturgical, and creedal formulations. We have also learned the price of not distinguishing cultural values and assumptions from the gospel. (It was unfortunate that, four centuries ago, Matco Ricci did not receive permission to employ Chinese rites when his mission to China was almost off the ground.) We have a better grasp today of the diversity within the New Testament writings, and share the historical consciousness characteristic of the twentieth century.

But if one means whether people today can sin against the light, the answer, sadly, is yes.

Footnotes to the Appendix

1. International Theological Commission, "Theses on the Relationship between the Ecclesiastical Magisterium and Theology" (United States Catholic Conference, 1977), p. 9.

2. See Bernard Lonergan, *The Way to Nicea: The*

Dialectical Development of Trinitarian Theology (Philadelphia, 1976), p. 13ff.

3. Léon Cristiani, *Heresies and Heretics* (New York, 1959), p. 11. This is volume 136 of *The Twentieth Century Encyclopedia of Catholicism*.

4. St. Hilary of Poitiers, *De Trinitate,* Book 2, Chapter 2, as cited by Maurice Wiles in *The Making of Christian Doctrine* (Cambridge, 1967), pp. 32-33.

5. See Gordon Leff, *Heresy in the Later Middle Ages* (New York, 1967), vol. 1, pp. 4-5.